Echoes of Nature

A Poetry Collection

Bonnie R. Sargent

LAKE SOLITUDE MEDIA | CASPER WY

Echoes of Nature: A Poetry Collection
Copyright © 2022 by Bonnie R. Sargent

Photos from Unsplash.com or taken by Gayle M. Irwin. All rights reserved. No part of this publication may be reproduced, distributed or transmitted in any form or by any means, without prior written permission.

Publisher:
Lake Solitude Media
1622 South Oak St.
Casper, WY 82601

Echoes of Nature – A Poetry Collection
Bonnie R. Sargent -- 1st ed.

Dedication

I dedicate this poetry collection to all the dogs in my life
who have kept me young and humble
and given me inspiration.
– Bonnie R. Sargent

*Poetry is when an emotion has found its thought
and the thought has found words.*
– Robert Frost

SOURCE: BRAINY QUOTE.COM

Table of Contents

SECTION 1 Nature 1
    Alpine Meadow 2
    The Raindrop 4
    Midnight Peace 6
    Lookout Point 7
    Silver Lining 8
    Emergence 9
    Weeds 11
    Flower Feud 12
    My Garden Sanctuary 13
    My Hide-Away 14
    Nature Haiku: A Collection 16
    rain writing 18
    Out of the Ashes 20
    Pulling Weeds 22
    Rain on the Windshield 25
    River Distractions 26
    River of Life 29
    The Dragonfly 30
    The Mountain 32
    The River 34
    The Thunderstorm 35

Violent Poem	37
Peaceful Poem	38
Water	39
We Are Wyoming	40
SECTION 2 Animals	43
A Boy and His Dog	44
Bascombe the Basset Hound	46
Breakfast at the Hunting Camp	47
Animal Spirit	48
Empty Nest Syndrome	50
Dog Droppings	51
If I Were a Dog	53
The Art of Raising a Basset Hound	55
Nighttime Kiss	56
Remembrance	57
Home Sweet Home	58
The Broken Sparrow	59
Tiger On the Hunt	60
Unwelcome Rain	61
River Side Blessing	62
Swimming with the Koi	64
SECTION 3 Seasons	67
Season to Season	68
Autumn Pageantry	69

Springtime Celebration	70
Gathering	71
March Winds	72
Peaks and Valleys	73
Rebirth	77
Springtime	79
Summer Solace	80
That Time of Year	81
Tree of New Beginnings	83
Winter Tantrum	85
SECTION 4 Faith	86
God and Nature	87
Eye-to-Eye With God	88
Angels in Disguise	90
Country Cemetery	92
God's Plan	93
Seeing-Eye God	95
Soul-ward Bound	96
The Rainbow Bridge	97
Well- Being	100
About the Author	102
About the Book	103

SECTION 1

Nature

Nature inspires me. Living in Wyoming, I'm surrounded by nature, from mountains and plains to my home's garden and flower beds. I've rafted the Colorado River, made trips to Yellowstone National Park, and national forests and monuments. Stars blanketed me and wildflower meadows embraced me. Whether I'm in the wilderness or sitting near the pond in my backyard, nature fills my senses and enriches my soul.

Alpine Meadow

Atop the craggy mountain,
far above the valley floor,
lies a meadow graced with flowers,
which my heart can just adore.

Every color in the rainbow,
dots the grassland all around.
Every color God created
in wild profusion does abound.

I imagine my creator,
after six exhausting days,
wanted nothing but to rest awhile,
but He knew He must amaze.

He took His artist's pallet,
put on a paint dab of each hue.
They he spun it all around,
flinging yellow, red, and blue.

Each place the paint touched down
became a lovely flower.
He looked around and nodded,
then sent a gentle shower.

When His work was finally finished,
He wiped his pallet on the sky,
creating the first rainbow,
a pleasure to the eye.

Each spring when winter wanes,
and springtime warms the land,
we're reminded of the artwork
that's created by God's hand.

When the meadow is in flower,
we're reminded of the gift
that God created for us,
our heavy hearts to lift.

When I begin to mull it over,
I think that is the reason
why springtime is my favorite,
and is such a lovely season.

BONNIE R. SARGENT

The Raindrop

One raindrop merged with countless others,
ran rivulets down the windowpane.
Streaking the window, they distorted the view,
as if looking through a magnifying glass.

Who could tell from mere gazing
which would feed a starving flower?
Which would merely drown the unwary?
Raindrops, be they friend or foe?

A gusty breeze thrust a single raindrop
onto my threshold and through the door.
Of the countless tiny missiles falling from the sky,
why that one raindrop?

Of numberless openings into buildings,
why was mine the chosen one?
The light from within my home
shone no brighter than others in the storm.

Of all the many raindrops
that could have entered my door,
You are the one that was sent,
and ushered in on a breeze.

There is no doubt in my mind
just whose breath you rode upon.
Tears of gratitude flow like rivulets
down the windowpanes of my heart.

I know not why you chose me
to lavish your care upon.
All I can offer is a heartfelt "Thank you,"
for your droplet nourishes me so.

Midnight Peace

A gibbous moon illuminates the face of the sky,
with a dusting of thin clouds to powder its nose.
A gentle breeze cools my day-heated face
and ruffles the pine tree, as if it were my hair.

Pin-pricks of starlight gleam upon the sky
like a dusting of freckles across my cheek.
The gentle pealing of a wind chime
sings lullabies to the heart of this restless soul.

Even though the day has been long,
with cares and duties needing attending,
the dark seems to wipe clean yesterday's slate.
Tomorrow will begin clean, bathed in newness.

I have long been a creature of the night.
My rhythm quickens with the setting of the sun.
I have made the darkness my friend,
and watch the dawn with a feeling of resignation.

Lookout Point

High on a hill overlooking the town
lays the most beautiful place ever found.
A person can see for miles and miles,
an experience surely to bring on smiles.

The sky seems to stretch on, never to stop.
To the ground is a tremendous drop.
There is a fence to keep you from falling,
a disaster that would be most appalling!

A river runs across the valley floor,
making a picture like never before.
On Saturday night it is crowded, but heck!
That's where the teenagers all go to neck.

Silver Lining

When clouds are thick and black,
too dense for eyes to pierce,
when thunder rends the sky,
and lightning strikes are fierce,

while creatures bolt in terror,
to flee the mighty storm,
that's when a shelter finds you,
to keep you safe and warm.

With lightning comes the rainfall,
to nurture all the Earth.
Behind it comes the sunshine,
with stirrings of rebirth.

When trouble comes a knocking,
and for peace your heart is pining,
reach through the wall of clouds,
and touch the silver lining.

Emergence

The sun emerges from its winter rest,
bathing the earth with warmth so blessed.
Under the layer of frozen snow
the signs of spring begin to grow.

Rivulets of cold water trickle,
playing games with the sun so fickle.
Hide and seek is the game they play,
Shouting "Catch me if you may!"

It wakens the sleeping buds of trees,
who say "Come catch me, if you please."
The bulbs in the ground raise sleepy heads
and leave their sodden wintery beds.

The grass on the hillsides begins to green
as soon as longer days are seen.
Each baby sleeping in its mother's womb,
begins to feel a lack of room.

"I want to come outside to play!"
each infant shouts as it makes its way.
Each critter growing inside an egg
enters the world on shaky leg.

The scent of blossoms fills the air,
with jonquils and daffodils everywhere.
Grape hyacinths are on parade,
dotting purple the sleepy glade.

As the air begins to warm,
honeybees begin to swarm.
Birds return from their long migration,
ready for a long vacation.

People, eager for the warmth to come,
indulge in exercising their green thumb.
Just as our hearts begin to thump,
nature delivers a big snow dump!

Weeds

The weeds in my garden shout defiance at me.
Where there is one, there soon will be three.
Do I destroy them because they are wild.
If that is the case, then what of that child?

The one I once was, who gave parents grief.
I'd have been plucked from the tree like a leaf.
Instead of attacking all those errant weeds,
I gently cultivate to meet all their needs.

They're given a chance to grow, just as I,
to rise up tall, as they stretch toward the sky.
The neighbors declare that I have a green thumb,
as I dig in the earth, to their praise I succumb.

Flower Feud

Flower bed, shaped like a dog bone,
filled with frozen flowers and vines.
"I can't believe she won't give us water,"
Delphinium sighs and then whines.

"Are you nuts?" asks the Cone Flower.
"Water would freeze head to foot."
"Then you'd turn black as midnight,
right down to your dyed purple root."

A pansy enters the squabble,
glaring with black, blazing eyes.
"Just wait for her to come trim you.
She'll cut you right down to size."

"Mum, Pansy's being mean to us!
Would you please make her quit?"
Mum says, "You all just hush up,
or I'll tell her to pour on bull shit!"

"All right," they all grumble sulking,
"I guess that won't do any harm.
It'll just make us grow taller,
and we all know that fertilizer's warm."

My Garden Sanctuary

What is it about a garden space
that makes it seem such a welcome place?
Troubles seem to just fade away
whenever I go to that place to pray.

Flowers seem to absorb my sorrow;
help me to see a brighter tomorrow.
Bees hum, inspecting each flower,
seeming to grant me infinite power.

The sun brightly shines down on me,
making me feel I'm where I should be.
Every rainbow color abounds,
making my garden an enchanted grounds.

Whenever a plant, into the soil I dig
it takes on new life, making it big.
Each plant or rock, so lovingly laid,
makes me strong, so I'm not afraid.

When sorrow finds its way to me,
I have protection, as you can see.
It surrounds me, and grants a pardon
whenever I come to my lovely garden.

My garden is there for all who come,
be he a prince or a homeless bum.
Peace from my garden, you can see,
doesn't require a pedigree.

My Hide-Away

Nestled against a backdrop of green
lies the most beautiful sight I've seen.
It isn't fancy or spun with gold.
In fact, it's drafty and kind of old.

The chimney crumbles, the flue has a draft.
But it makes me want to ply my craft.
As I look out on the glistening lake,
I feel God's bounty, and I want to partake.

A meadowlark trills its lovely song,
and the words I pen can do no wrong.
The mountains seem to reach the sky,
and make me feel that I can fly!

Out in the lake jumps a rainbow trout,
making the words I have leap out.
A squirrel chitters from up in a tree,
saying that it believes in me.

This little log cabin, hardly a shack,
makes my need to write come back.
I don't understand. It makes no sense!
A pathway beckons through woods so dense.

How can I follow the curlew's cry,
or watch clouds building in the sky?
How can I write a decent verse
when the call of the wild is such a curse?

I guess I have an age-old quandary;
do I throw clothes away or do my laundry?
How on earth am I to fight it?
Should I live life to full, or take time to write it?

Nature Haiku: A Collection

Brook, laugh at nothing.
Embrace this God-Given day.
Purify your soul.

Sun, on bended back,
warm this man's arthritic bones.
Sleep, old grizzly, sleep.

Creep softly, chipmunk.
Sidle into my presence.
Wink at me, and scold.

Sap-like, down a tree
nectar of the honeybee
rapture for bear tongue

Nestled at your feet,
sing a lullaby to comfort,
Ponderosa Pine.

Like a speck of dust
settling on a table,
flies arrive for lunch.

Happy hiker shouts,
you are the voice of summer,
that groans with each step home.

Symphony of stars,
like fire flies a'dancing
upon the black sky

I grieve, fallen tree
that tragedy befell you.
Should I pray for you?

Chipmunk feet scurry,
leave footprints up my backbone,
icicles of fear.

rain writing

back porch under tin roof
cushioned chair
journal propped on crossed knees
pencil between teeth
as if they could bite the words out

mother of pearl sky
gusty winds
flap pages of journal
as if impatient for words
that refuse to come

gusts grow stronger
sky darkens into a bad mood
bolt of lightning
roll of thunder
spatter of raindrops

black clouds boil overhead
sky erupts into maelstrom
of rain wind lightning thunder
weeping clouds soak ground
rain gods are angry

tin roof like pounding hoofs
as storm stampedes across sky
downspouts overflow
hail bounces high off lawn
needles rip from pine tree

stampede fades into distance
rain slows then stops
wind dies to stillness
air laundered to freshness
storm is no more

words spew onto page
like rain from clouds
emptying the soul
and leaving peace
the storm is gone

Out of the Ashes

A tree stands alone in the forest,
branches nearly denuded,
soot-blackened, reminders of sparks
carelessly loosed by a passerby.
The choking underbrush of seasons past
is but a memory.
The sun greets the tree, as it raises its uppermost branches
in acceptance.

Forgotten are the daily struggles for a few sunbeams,
snatched from the grasp of other forest trees.
The choking vines, bushes, and bramble
that leeched nourishment from the soil,
are all gone now.

Where once the forest crowded out all view,
now the tree's whole mountainside
spreads in panoramic splendor.
Fresh new grasses and mountain flowers
carpet the ground at its roots.

Some shy away, fearful that damage
might somehow befall them,
or shield the tree, convinced the damaged one
cannot stand by itself.
In doing so, they block the healing rays of the sun
from the recovering tree.

Those few, whose uppermost branches
rise above the canopy,
see clearly enough to recognize
the enhanced perspective of the lone tree.
These few lean close, hoping to catch a glimpse
of what the blackened tree sees.

We are one with the trees of the forest.
Which are you?
Which am I?

Pulling Weeds

My evening passed just pulling weeds
that grew in wild profusion
around my yard, in flower beds,
a tangle of confusion.

Now most folks balk at pulling weeds,
for many a different reason.
Some claim it's a boring way
to pass the summer season.

Others say hay fever strikes
with speed like a charging bull,
the moment they even touch a weed,
or give the slightest pull.

I'm quite content to sit me down
amidst the noxious plants,
despite the risk of grass stains
on the seat of my garden pants.

Enjoyment comes from ripping roots
right out of protesting ground.
Those weeds had better watch their step
whenever I'm around!

I have my favorite kinds of weeds,
the ones real big around,
for once you wrench them from their spot
you've really cleared some ground.

The hardest ones for me to face,
are the ones you can hardly see.
When you pluck one gently from its bed,
the clearing is too small for me.

It's really tempting just to skip
those wimpy little rascals.
But sure as shooting, if you do
you're asking for fiascos.

No sooner have you gone inside
than those weedlings begin to grow.
They loom up large, and fill your yard
and you don't even know.

Just like weeds in your garden,
the unwanted seeds of your mind
take root in the dark and damp places
of your soul, making it blind.

It seems, like the weeds in a garden,
our troubles are varied and many.
They often grow thick and rank.
Seldom are there not any.

One might think the big sort of troubles
would be the hardest to solve.
But often big problems are mastered
by just one hard yank of resolve.

Instead it's those woes that start out
so small that we don't even see,
that quietly grow into jungles
so thick that we only can flee.

Heed the advice of this gardener:
Experience has taught me one thing:
Take care of your weeds both large and small,
and see what bounty you'll bring.

Rain on the Windshield

Tiny spots of rain cover the windshield,
like marks of a Braille machine gone mad.
Is my life written in the sprinkles,
spelling out what the future has in store?

Have I time to decipher the words,
before the wipers swipe them away?
Do I read with my eyes, or my fingers?
Braille is not a visual art.

Likewise, life is often not clearly seen,
but must be touched and caressed.
Should I welcome the rain that falls,
spelling out the Braille message of life?

Rain often refreshes an outlook
that has become dusty and withered.
Sometimes the sun shines so brightly
that sprinkles of rain disappear into thin air.

Do not become so enamored with sunshine
you fail to read the message of rain-times.
Life is not complete without sun and rain.
Cherish each, for they nourish one other.

River Distractions

I wanted to write a poem about
a beautiful magenta Geranium,
but was distracted by a tree root
nibbling at my toe.

I wanted to write a poem about a feathery,
lime-green fern kissing the surface of the water,
but was distracted by a tree root
tugging at my shoelaces.

I wanted to write a poem about a gnarled, twisted,
majestic old fir tree, but was distracted by a tree root,
its witch-like fingers snagging my socks.

I wanted to write a poem about the Merganser
and her furry babies,
dabbing about on the far side of the stream,
but was distracted by a tree root
wrapping around my ankle and refusing to let go.

I wanted to write a poem about a place
where a squirrel prepared a feast
for its wedding reception on a tree stump,
but was distracted by a tree root that
just about detached my kneecap.

I wanted to write a poem about the mighty roar of
the mountain stream as it frothed angrily on its way
down the mountain, but was distracted by a tree root
that coiled right up my leg and extracted
my last Snickers bar from my back pocket.

I wanted to write a poem about a frail blue Gentian
growing among the brambles on a steep mountainside,
but was distracted by a damn tree root
that reached right up and unzipped my pants,
causing me to get a mosquito bite.

I wanted to write a poem about that mosquito bite,
but was distracted by a frail Blue Gentian
with gossamer butterfly wing petals, growing among
the brambles on a steep mountainside.

I wanted to write about that Snickers bar,
but was distracted by a mighty river, roaring its displeasure
at my intrusion, as it hurled its way down the mountainside.

I wanted to write a poem about my kneecap,
but was distracted by a tree stump,
where I imagined a squirrel had prepared
a feast for its wedding reception.

I wanted to write about my ankle,
but was distracted by a Merganser mama
and her downy babies, dabbing about in search of tidbits
in the ripples on the far bank of the stream.

BONNIE R. SARGENT

I wanted to write a poem about my socks,
but was distracted by a majestic, twisted,
and gnarled old fir tree, standing proud and tall,
despite its arthritic branches and great age.

I wanted to write a poem about my shoelaces,
but was distracted by a feathery, lime green fern,
bending low as if in prayer,
kissing the surface of the water.

I wanted to write a poem about my toes,
but was distracted by a radiant, magenta Geranium,
clinging stoically to life on an eroding bank
of the mountain stream.

I wanted to write!

River of Life

A river is born
small and insignificant.
High up in the mountain
it spews out from deep
beneath the surface of the earth.

Like the river,
we humans also spew out
from deep within
the Mother's womb.
Small and insignificant,
we too must carve a path.

As it journeys down the mountain,
the river builds up force.
Its growing strength
carves out solid rock,
building a pathway.

As the stream continues
down the mountainside,
it grows in size and power.
It gathers sand and rocks
to help it etch its way.

Growing children must also
gather materials for tools.
Learning provides the power
for them to carve their own way
down the mountainside of life.

The Dragonfly

A dragonfly nearly three inches long
lit upon my hand.
The breeze from the river
sent its translucent wings
to shimmering in silver splendor.
Its long, slender body shone
like a periwinkle gemstone.
As I gazed upon the dragonfly
against the wrinkled,
age spotted hand it perched upon,
I felt envy for this creature
that God chose to bless
with such a stream-lined,
colorful body.

Then it disappeared into the swarm
hovering over the surface of the living river.
Within a few minutes,
another dragonfly took its place
on my hand.
Or was it the first one,
back again to rest its wings upon me?
I couldn't tell for sure,
judging from my human,
untrained eye.

I looked out
at the group of women
with whom I travelled.
Not a gemstone body
or shimmering wing
existed in my human population,
but we humans had something precious
that the beautiful dragonfly lacked —
individuality.
I was no longer envious.

The Mountain

It wasn't particularly tall,
as far as mountains go.
And the meadow on its top
was nearly devoid of snow.

The rugged face of the mountain
showed years of wind and ice,
carving it into a sculpture.
Its creases made me look twice.

Its foothills and up its slope,
stood sturdy, proud and strong.
I studied the mountain in detail,
knowing it had been there long.

The mountain wasn't newly formed.
It had been there a while.
There was just something about it
that made me want to smile.

The creatures beneath its branches
lived a life devoid of fear.
The mountain met all their needs,
giving shelter to them here.

The mountain seemed to reach out
gathering me to its heart.
I knew from that day forth,
I'd never want to part.

I'd spend my days with its forest
enclosing me all around.
I'd listen to its bubbling brooks,
a most alluring sound

I'd sleep beneath its deep sky
and watch its stars shine brightly.
I'd pray to my God above,
and thank Him for it nightly.

He wasn't particularly tall,
as far as humans go.
And the meadow on his top
was nearly devoid of snow.

The River

The river hurries by
in a never-ending rush to the sea.
Does it never grow weary
knowing that's the way it must be?

Does the water ever marvel
as it passes under sheer, rocky cliffs?
Does it ever pray to the river god,
thanking him for many wondrous gifts?

Does the river feel insignificant
when endless sky fills with countless stars?
Or does it look beyond the night,
wondering if what it sees is Mars?

How does the river stay humble
knowing how it can touch our souls?
Does it raise its head in pride,
or set itself some rather lofty goals?

I think the river mighty
from the time it's just a trickling stream,
up to the time it's made it to the sea
fulfilling every river's fondest dream.

The Thunderstorm

Afternoon waxed hot and sultry,
sweat beading my brow like rain on a window.
Dark clouds scudded the horizon,
harbingers of doom to come.

Horses in the corral paced nervously,
ready to spook at nothing.
Breath fought to remain in my chest,
unwilling to leave its protection.

Air drooped motionless in the trees,
too weak to stir the leaves.
Birds sagged on the branches,
waiting, for what, they knew not.

Scream of wind down the draw,
yanking leaves into a vortex
of swirling, whirling confusion.
A nightmare awakened and set free.

Bright light slashed the heavens,
followed by a drumroll of sound.
The cabin quaked, then settled,
used to rampage of temper from the sky.

Deafening crack ripped the ozone,
searing the edges of my hearing.
I sought refuge in the dark,
arms locked around the quaking dog.

Eternity came and went in an hour,
while rain poured off the roof.
Tension dissolved like a backrub,
leaving the world a fresher place.

Violent Poem

The river thrashes, screaming its rage.
It fights itself as if in a cage.
Water batters eroding banks,
like raking spurs along its flanks.

Spray flies up like a foaming beast,
with anger centuries have never ceased.
The battle rages from dusk till dawn,
and once again till the sun is gone.

The cliffs crowd in pressing for control.
Water rushes through, escape its only goal.
The water so hates to be contained
it rushes on and on, its anger never drained.

Peaceful Poem

Miles downriver, the valley gets wide,
and the anger of the river goes away to hide.
The current gets slower, the water gets calm.
It soothes the soul like an aloe balm.

The cliffs recede, giving the river room,
to float on gently, as if in the womb.
Freedom gives the channel a way to survive,
happy and content, glad to be alive.

Mankind could take a lesson from the river.
One that Mother Nature would surely deliver.
The soul needs room to expand and grow.
Too much crowding turns it into a foe.

Water

Water can save our lives,
and also wash us away.
It can clean the air,
or turn the sky to gray.

Water has different voices.
singing songs of joy.
It can relax and soothe us,
make sailors shout "Ahoy!"

Rain can pound in a fury.
Arroyos can fill in a flash,
tearing out trees and eroding,
carrying critters and trash.

I've listened to rain on a tent roof,
as well as a burbling brook.
I've stood by the waves in the ocean,
never tiring of the look.

I don't want to live on Pluto,
or even as close as Mars.
The rain wouldn't be there,
to clean windshields on cars!

We Are Wyoming

We're sturdy purple sage that blankets the rocky hill,
and songs of meadowlarks that warm the morning chill.
We're rumbling thunderheads in black and lowering skies,
and crooning of night hawks that once closed cattle's eyes.

We're ghosts of long-gone bison that filled the golden plain,
and the ever-working farmer planting rich, black fields with grain.
We're vibrant Indian Paint Brush dotting mountain slopes
with red, and the single, lonely grave where some pioneer
laid his dead.

We're the mighty, soaring eagle as she rides the indigo sky,
and enormous cottonwoods whose limbs reach oh, so high.
Sagebrush, meadowlark, night hawk, farmer,
paint brush, cottonwood,
each makes our souls much warmer.

All these things, we are!

We're great wide-open range before barbed wire cut the land,
and an old-time working cowboy with his willing calloused hand.
We're ever-present wind
soughing through lonesome valleys,
and a smooth-handed sheep man
with his clippers and his tallies.

We're open, friendly faces of people living here,
where love and human-kindness
are not trodden out by fear.
We're Tetons and Rockies that shape horizons far,
and inky black of nighttime,
lit up by a billion stars.

We're rich, thick veins of coal hiding beneath the soil,
and oil field pumps and gushers
saving mankind endless toil.
Open range, calloused hands,
shepherds with their flocks,
mountains, night skies, and get-to-know-you talks.

All these things, we are!

We're pristine mountain lakes,
and streams that run so clear
to see them brings such gladness,
you're like to shed a tear.
We're ever-changing weather,
fickle as a woman,
and wolves in Yellowstone,
brought back there by some humans.

We're vast and empty spaces,
with air so light and clean,
and so sparse a population, oft-times others can't be seen.
We're geysers spewing water
in wondrous Yellowstone,
and famous Devil's Tower,
with legends all its own.

We're spirit of grizzly,
and majesty of Bighorn Sheep
ranging through lodge pole pine, and up mountainsides so steep.
Lakes, streams, grizzlies and mountain sheep,
Yellowstone geysers, Devil's Tower, and restful, peaceful sleep.

All these things, we are!

We're the voice of days gone by and of how life is today.
We're keepers of legends, and of memories along the way.
The most important thing we are, or that we've ever done,
We are Wyoming's people.
Be proud and say "I'm one."

SECTION 2
Animals

Animals also inspire and impact me. From wildlife found in nature to pets living in homes, animals touch our lives in positive and delightful ways! Childhood memories and adult experiences with animals increase our compassion and layer our souls with love … if we open our hearts.

BONNIE R. SARGENT

A Boy and His Dog

A boy and his dog are a marvelous pair,
lavishing love, and kisses and care.
They find adventures to fill their days.
One of them leads and the other obeys.

None is more important to a boy,
for filling his life with a fullness of joy.
A dog helps him learn how to take and to give,
making his life so much better to live.

A boy doesn't need an expensive gift
to make his heart soar and ready to lift
out of the mundane and into the light.
A dog can make his world seem right.

One thing on which we all can agree –
the dog doesn't need a pedigree.
Any old mutt will do just fine.
It doesn't matter which breeds combine.

A child can learn loyalty by example,
from his dog, whose gifts are ample.
He can learn compassion and how to care,
how to give, and how to be fair.

There is no highly educated teacher,
nor even a very Godly preacher,
who can guide a boy into being a man,
as well as his trusty side-kick can.

If you have a boy without a pet,
it isn't too late to fix it yet.
Just get him a dog and you will see
how very happy you both will be.

Bascombe the Basset Hound

He came to me through a rescue group,
from an owner who wouldn't clean up his poop.
Big and brown, with a saddle that was black,
he entered my home, and rolled onto his back.

"Please rub my belly," his somber eyes implored.
I looked deep into them, and instantly adored.
I named him Bascombe, from a school book I read.
Before I knew what happened, he was sharing my bed.

He earned a nickname, which he kept forever:
Butthead......which he didn't get for being clever!
That dog was stubborn, worse than a mule.
Getting him to mind just made you feel a fool.

When you opened the door, he took off for the hills,
with me running wildly, giving even greater thrills.
I threatened not to follow, to just let him go.
I didn't mean it, and Bascombe seemed to know.

He had a little trick, which he never seemed to miss.
He'd wait for open mouth, and give a sloppy kiss.
When I forgot my keys, an event I learned to dread,
I'd crawl through the dog door, and he'd roll on my head!

I have often wondered just what I found so sweet,
in a rough and stubborn dog with such gigantic feet.
Perhaps it was because of his stubborn, loving heart.
Although he is long gone, we shall never part.

Breakfast at the Hunting Camp

I've never been much of a hunter.
I simply can't aim at a deer.
I probably make you all wonder
just why I want to be here.

I love to watch the sun rise,
above the hills to the east.
The smell of coffee boiling
is a sure sign there'll soon be a feast.

As eggs sputter in a skillet,
and taters turn to hash browns,
there are many loud yawns,
but seldom will you ever see frowns.

I listen and hear them approach,
and enter the camp like they own it.
Three little pot-bellied pigs
are demanding their morning donut.

Animal Spirit

river trip, Colorado River,
floating the current in river raft
scenery slipping by,
better than a moving picture

Sky haunting, beautiful blue,
cotton ball clouds here and there
float silently by
temporary respite from sun

as day fades to twilight,
we land on river bank
clamber from rafts,
eager to set up camp

from this moment on,
my movements change
from easy, to struggle
over rocks and deep sand

hardship won't stop
until on river once more
I flounder gracelessly through camp
eagerly awaiting morning

contemplation sings a lullaby,
of a sea lion's double life;
on land, floundering,
every move a struggle

in the sea, graceful and swift
moving easily through the waves
does he dread his time on land?
relish his ocean-time?

We have similar circumstances,
sea lion and I.
He helps me understand.
He is my animal spirit.

Empty Nest Syndrome

Six baby ducks came to live in our pond.
As I watched them grow, I became very fond.
At first, they looked like ping-pong balls,
with downy soft feathers and peeping calls.

Up and down the stream they bobbed.
Their mother had died. I felt they'd been robbed
of all the care that a mother gave.
We worked very hard, those six to save.

Many an hour I watched each antic,
when they were calm, or even frantic.
They came to follow us all around,
eating each sweet morsel they found.

At last they outgrew the room that we had.
We had to move them, which made me sad.
We transplanted them to a nearby pond,
leaving them there and breaking the bond.

It reminded me of the sorrow we face
when our kid moves out to get his own place.
I think the phrase that describes it best,
is that I suffer from an empty nest.

Dog Droppings

I drop down upon one knee, to hug his shaggy neck.
He covers me with hair again, but I think, "What the heck."
If that's all I can care about, then I'm a total wreck.

I learned this lesson years ago, when he was just a pup.
It doesn't matter what he's done. The mess will all clean up.
The love that he gives back to me o'erflows the biggest cup.

He drops the paper at my feet, and doesn't read it first.
He drops a treasure in my lap, so proud his heart could burst.
The mangled body of a mouse, his offering, well-rehearsed.

He sits there in front of me, a sock between his teeth.
He looks so very proud of what he's about to bequeath.
He finally found that sock that the bed tucked underneath.

"Drop it, boy!" I say to him, and watch the stocking fall.
His eyes grow sad, as do mine, I know he gave his all.
His tail grows still, and I see, I made the wrong call.

I'll try to make it up to him, we'll play his special game.
I'll feed him yummy treats today, 'cause I'm the one to blame.
I wish I could send that "Drop it," right back from whence it came.

"Drop it, boy," is what he heard, all the time he was a pup.
"Drop that shoe," "Drop that brush," and "Drop that coffee cup."
I had to say, "Drop it!" before he chewed it up.

That playful little puppy's gone, I guess he got dropped too.
I think of him, and want to cry, it makes me feel so blue.
He's grown into this loving dog, whose heart's so brave and true.

If I could tell him "Drop it!" again, I'd have him drop the years.
I'd have him drop those aching legs, and those Siren calls he hears.
Then I would drop, and hold him tight, as the Angel of Death appears.

If I Were a Dog

If I were a Basset Hound,
my ears would drag the ground.
My nose and tail would be far apart,
a good predicament if I had to fart.

A Jack Russell Terrier has get up and go,
If I were one, I'd be too slow.
If you want calm, don't make the error
of bringing home a Jack Russell Terror.

A Chihuahua is a tiny little pet,
about the smallest you can get.
He's such a cute, tiny pup,
that he will fit right in a cup.

I'd like being a Golden Retriever.
They are so gentle, you become a believer
in having a dog to share your life
be you child, husband or wife.

I would make a lousy Pekinese.
My fly-away hair would make me sneeze.
My upturned sinuses wouldn't drain,
and I might drown if caught in the rain.

A Dachshund might be my breed of choice,
but I'd have an awfully shrill little voice.
I'd also be so close to the floor,
Mom wouldn't have to mop anymore.

I would make a good Pit Bull example,
my kindness and gentleness are ample.
People would have nothing to fear,
when this Pit Bull sauntered near.

Being a Bulldog would make me wheeze.
It's so sad they can't breathe with ease.
Their squished up noses look adorable,
but disfigure their sinuses something horrible.

I think I'd settle for being a mutt.
No matter the mix, I'd have a cute butt.
My heart would be purebred, can't you see?
You don't have to have a pedigree.

The Art of Raising a Basset Hound

The first decision you must make:
Puppy or grown dog.........no piece of cake!
Weigh each side, list pro and con.
Puzzle it out from dusk till dawn.

If you are young and full of zest,
a puppy just might suit you best.
If your years have slowed you down,
an older dog won't make you frown.

Regardless which basset you settle upon,
your carefree days are nearly gone.
Your hair will gray, and ulcers fester
when your basset begins to pester.

"Sit" and "stay" just meaningless words,
following commands is for the birds!
Expecting him to obey a master
simply means you're courting disaster.

Accept that allowances must be made,
no matter what the price you paid.
Heed the advice of which I speak!
No basset suits if you're a control freak!

Nighttime Kiss

The night sky
lies purple with moonlight.
I lie in my bed, eyes closed in sleep.

The soft tread
of feet in the hallway
makes promises to help pass the night.

My heart quakes
with anticipation.
My dreams are about to be answered!

Soft, sweet kiss
pressed gently on forehead,
a gift from my beloved basset.

Remembrance

He basks in the sun streaming in through the door.
He isn't as young as he was once before.
Dreaming of youth, which has now disappeared,
he breathes in the feeling of how he was cheered.

He was a guard dog for his friends on the farm,
making certain that they came to no harm.
He longs for those long-gone days from the past.
To those precious memories he will hold on fast.

Sunbeams give warmth sinking into his fur,
making exhaustion seem only a blur.
Forgotten are the nights of withering cold.
Only happy memories have a strong hold.

Why is it as we look back on our life,
that we forget all the times of great strife?
Perhaps it's because we wish only to hold
onto those times when we felt not so old.

Home Sweet Home

The larder in the squirrel's burrow
groans to overflowing.
Pine nuts, acorns, and sunflower seeds
set the squirrel's heart to glowing.

He knows that winter will be long
but he's not the least bit worried.
All summer long he did his job
as from ground to tree he scurried.

The cat that lives in his back yard
can chase him all it wants.
The squirrel chitters a mocking sound
as that feline menace he taunts.

His lady squirrel is burrowed down
awaiting a pink new litter.
When he thinks of becoming a dad,
his stomach feels all atwitter.

As snowflakes swirl around their nest
the squirrels cease to roam.
They snuggle into their cozy nest
that signals, "Welcome home."

The Broken Sparrow

She was a tiny sparrow
lying broken in her nest.
The only sign of life within,
a flutter in her chest.

Her feathers were all ragged,
and she was too weak to rise.
This bird too ill for beauty,
but for light within her eyes.

I gazed so deep within the orbs,
her soul was shown to me.
T'was not a broken bird I saw,
but a creature of rare beauty.

She answered every thought of what
I knew a bird to be.
A picture seared upon my mind,
a cherished memory.

This picture of God's making
Will stay with me 'til the end.
This broken, lovely sparrow
whom I'm proud to count my friend.

BONNIE R. SARGENT

Tiger On the Hunt

She steals through the steamy jungle as quietly as a thought.
Other creatures quake in terror,
until her shadow disappears in the murky undergrowth.
Her eyes plumb the darkness in search of an unwary soul.
Tiger is on the hunt.

Hidden away from prying eyes,
her cubs search blindly for their mother's breast,
Unaware that a few short months away,
their own search for prey will begin,
as tigers on the hunt.

The mother feasts on the prey she brought down
in a maelstrom of fear and agony.
Thus sustained, she retires to her den
to minister to the needs of her young.
Her cubs are on the hunt.

In the den, the tigress gently grooms her cubs,
tongue rasping over their soft, silky hair.
She is as gentle as any mother with her young.
Such a contrast is her behavior toward other species,
as a tiger on the hunt.

We humans have much in common with the tiger.
We also can be brutal toward other species.
The difference is that we do it for sport, not just survival.
For a trophy on the wall, a trinket of ivory, bragging rights,
we humans are on the hunt.

Unwelcome Rain

The day grieved and shed its tears,
and felt like it would weep for years.
Such mean words did the black sky say!
Why must it always be this way?

She crouched there in abject pain,
and watched runnels of falling rain,
gathering on the window sill.
Violent trembling made her ill.

Thunder made her quake in fear,
unwelcome assault against her ear.
Was there a place out of harm's way?
Would she ever survive this day?

She heard the front door open wide.
She felt her savior come inside.
Out she slipped from her hiding place,
leaping and licking her master's face.

Strong arms gathered her within,
making her feel safe again.
Breathing evened, heartbeat slowed.
She much preferred that it had snowed!

River Side Blessing

The river was placid,
but downstream we knew
how her heart would be racing
and how her rapids grew.
She would change from the Mother,
asleep in her bed
to a lioness roaring,
turning men's hearts to dread.

Excitement engulfed us,
but underneath was fear.
Intently we listened,
straining every cell to hear
as our guides instructed
how to ride the Mother's breast,
how we all would get through
if we gave it our best.

About to embark,
we were surprised by a guest,
who fluttered into camp,
and alit on my chest,
An emerald green hummer,
less than two inches long,
He perched there, content,
surveying our throng.

He hopped to my hand,
which was close to my face,
looking deep in my eyes.
I could feel his grace.
"Safe journey," he blessed me,
reassurance, he gave.
The hummingbird passed on,
so tiny, so brave!

Each traveler was similarly
blessed by this bird.
He made not a sound,
but we believed every word.
Safe passage downriver was wild,
it was thrilling!
I shall see him again,
to give thanks, God willing.

Swimming with the Koi

I've often wondered
what it would be like
to be a Koi.

In the winter time
while the fish lie dormant
in the frozen pond,

I've wondered what it must feel like.
I feel the blood
as it thickens and slows.

I perceive my breath
slowing down and getting shallow.
I feel as if I am drifting.

As the dark, cold days
marched on one following another
I wait patiently for life to begin anew.

Life must feel fleeting
when you are a Koi,
forced to wait for the sun

to bring you back to life.
How fickle that heavenly orb,
granting or withholding warmth!

Oh, but then the absolute joy
of life quickening in blood vessels,
with the coming of summer!

As babies hatch and plants grow,
the blood quickens,
thrumming through sleeping veins!

Bodies burst with energy,
and stomachs roar with hunger!
Now is the time for life!

As the Koi float and weave
through the moving water,
setting about nature's chores,

The pond seethes with life,
as dragon flies dart overhead
flirting with death by Koi.

Do the fish notice the solitary figure
quietly watching them
as they go about their ways?

I am that solitary figure.
Do the fish perceive me as a threat,
or understand my act of love?

I have often dreamed of being a Koi
living in our fish pond.
As I swam beneath the lily pads,

what would they look like underneath?
Would they be smooth, or veined,
with stems rising up like a teeming jungle?

As the water chilled my skin,
would I hear the constant rumble
of water flowing through?

That constant noise might bother me,
or might I not notice it,
having never known quiet?

Did I know what a serene home I had,
the beauty surrounding me,
or that I was cherished?

I have never experienced being a Koi.
I have never even waded in the pond,
or felt the coldness of the water.

Why do I feel so at one with the Koi?
Good imagination helps a lot,
hours of observation also!

What is the point
of this singular obsession?
I fear I am a little bit crazy!

SECTION 3
Seasons

Seasons of nature bring change, just as life brings change to us. Sometimes that change is welcome; many times, it is not. Yet, we can learn many lessons by experiencing the various seasons in nature just as we can learn lessons from the seasons, and changes, that come to us in life. Seasons bring a joyful dance as colorful leaves drift from trees or as light, buoyant snowflakes waft from the sky. Seasons can also bring fear as thunder and lightning rip across the sky, as wind howls and twists, as floodwaters roar, or as sun soaks moisture from the land like a child slurping through a straw. Change, seasons – a mixture of beauty and challenge.

Season to Season

When trees turn from green to red, yellow, and gold,
it tells of a never-ending cycle so bold.
Foreshadowing several months filled with cold,
when the warmth of the sun, God must withhold.

A promise of better days to come, the leaves tell.
The terrors of being forsaken they quell,
for how could we be destined to end up in Hell,
when to the ground such bright colors fell?

The colorful leaves promise warm days to come,
when through the air bees once more will hum.
Man need not be so frightened he's numb,
for destitute, God will not let us become.

When you see the autumn leaves starting to fall,
just find enough courage for you to stand tall.
Inside your warm home it's time now to crawl,
to bask in the safety God puts behind each wall.

After the long months of cold, God will bring
the promise of life with the coming of spring.
No longer must we, to our dark shelters cling.
Out into the sunlight, rejoicing we'll sing.

So when you see leaves on the trees start to turn,
do not let your heart begin to yearn.
From many past seasons of springtime we learn,
that once more the season of rebirth we'll earn.

Autumn Pageantry

Why do you hide your beauty from the eye
with summer garments all in somber hue?
Perhaps because you simply are too shy,
just knowing you cannot match heaven's blue.
Now that autumn-time has reached the hills,
you have matured beyond the summer's youth.
You proudly display petticoats and frills,
and radiant pigments that show you in truth.

Out Lady Aspen drapes in brilliant gold,
as old Sir Maple sports a crimson coat.
And Madame Buckeye finally can unfold
the silky orange so light it seems to float.
Of all the autumn glory in the land,
I love the seedling planted by my hand.

Springtime Celebration

As winter winds release their frigid air,
and life begins to quicken underground,
as sap begins to plump the branches bare,
I know that springtime soon will come around.

The buds swell slowly on each shapely limb,
like adolescent girls with budding breasts.
Our happy hearts can sing a joyous hymn
much like the robins singing in their nests.

Each unfurled leaf, perfection in the womb,
awaits the day when it can face the light.
And as its flowers open up in bloom,
it senses that its birthing time is right.

The springtime slowly turns a greenish hue,
and gives the gift of life to see us through.

Gathering

As summer draws to a close,
the pulse of the earth speeds ahead
as if to make up for a time
when land will turn drab and seem dead.

Bears feast on the last berries
falling overripe from the vine.
They claw up roots that are buried
and on the bounty they dine.

Squirrels, chipmunks, and mice
scurry over the harvested field,
gathering grains left by threshers,
to increase their winter's yield.

Shovels bite deep in the soil
gathering the garden plunder.
They dig up potatoes and turnips
before the snows seal them under.

We live in a world of procrastinators,
who wait until time runs short
before worrying about the future,
as if it's some kind of sport.

If warmth didn't lull us to linger
over leisure pursuits in the summer,
would we live a life less frantic?
Would we march to a different drummer?

March Winds

Why does March have the reputation
of hurling winds through this great nation?
"Go in like a lion; go out like a lamb,"
in many places is just a sham.

March has other famous times,
so let's not focus on just wind crimes.
The Ides of March you should beware.
Shakespeare told us to take a care.

Saint Patrick's Day is a March occurrence.
The "Luck of the Irish" gives assurance
that Christianity is alive and well
in Ireland or anyplace you dwell.

Pigs and peanut butter each have a day
set aside in March, or so they say.
There's even a March "Be Nasty Day."
Not too many observe that, I pray!

Sure, winds blow in early spring…
days in March that make us sing;
bringing in the warmer air,
that gives us comfort everywhere.

Peaks and Valleys

Have you noticed how our lives reflect
the silhouette of Earth
or how a tragic death is often followed
by a birth?
Did you know that we have seasons,
just as surely as does time,
or that they pass by rapidly,
like the gestures of the mime?

The spring of life is filled brimful of birth,
and childhood wonder.
As kids we have the heart to keep on trying
if we blunder.
Likewise, the grass upon the hill does not
lie dead and dormant.
It pushes up above the snow,
to let the sunshine warm it.

As young adults, our summer years are filled
with daily living.
There doesn't seem to be the time for loving,
or for giving.
We seem to gain much comfort
from maintaining status quo.
The peaks and valleys in our lives
are no longer where we go.

As autumn overtakes the land
and silences the thrumming,
we pause a moment, catch our breath,
and hear the earth's heart drumming.

It isn't racing wildly but has reached a steady pace.
It knows that "Easy does it, is the way to win the race.

Then icy winter chills the soul
and leaves its life behind.
It leaves its creatures on their own
to eat what they can find.

This season often is not kind,
but neither is it cruel.
To say how much we hate it
only makes us look a fool.

Spring is the highest mountain peak,
right after it was formed.
It looks inviting for we long to be
embraced and warmed.
The sunshine on the steeper cliffs
make vistas rather stunning.
With strength and willingness,
we take off toward them, running.

Summer is the wide plateau,
where hills are smaller features.
We tend to gaze out, straight ahead,
avoiding other creatures.
As thunderheads roll over plains
and distant echoes rumble,
We look ahead and crush the urge
to help others as they stumble.

Once again, as autumn comes,
the mountains reach new heights.
Gone are the fears of faster speeds,
as life takes lower flights.
The pathways can be strolled along,
without the fear of slipping.
And sluggish creeks of summer time,
run icy cold and dripping.

The deepest valleys, the winters of life,
come as death draws near.
We plummet to the valley floor,
where we likely break from fear.
This is the season we all dread,
as it represents our end.
Do not despair. Don't run away.
Just stop and think, my friend.

BONNIE R. SARGENT

If there were never any peaks or valleys in our lives,
The sameness would become a drudge,
like faceless, identical wives.
The journey through life would be a trip
through Kansas fields of wheat,
Where there's nothing to rest the eye,
just all one big repeat.

My choice for traveling through this life
would include the Rockies' peaks.
Death Valley also would be a goal,
where the ghost of yesteryear speaks.
A few wheat fields and fields of corn
would also enter in.
To give my soul a chance to rest,
and enjoy life, wherever it's been.

Rebirth

The heartbeat of the earth increases
as springtime draws ever nearer.
Gone are the days of gloomy dark.
Lost is the winter's furor.

Deep in its burrow a chipmunk stirs,
scrabbling through her larder.
She builds her nest with a single goal,
as birth pains grow ever harder.

The sap lying dormant in its trunk
quickens and begins to flow.
It may not seem that spring is here,
but somehow the tree gods know.

Icicles grow inexorably longer,
even though all winter they slept.
Under the snowdrifts water seeps,
as if The Mother has wept.

Day after day the sun shines down,
a bit warmer than the day before.
With hardly a warning of change to come,
winter is here no more.

What does it mean to two-footed creatures,
who have huddled in our lodging.
It means we are free to roam the land
with no more tempest dodging.

Spring gushes forth from the Mother's womb.
Her waters bring hope for us all.
The mad rush is on; she can't rest a day,
for on rushes summer and fall.

Springtime

Of all the seasons of the year,
I like spring the most.
It has a friendly, warming air,
with sunshine as its host.

The beauty of a budding leaf,
as it slowly comes to life,
reminds me of a pretty maid,
when she becomes a wife.

The sparkling of a bubbling stream,
all crowned with clean, white snow,
is such a good, refreshing scene,
I never want to go.

The coming of a newborn calf,
that runs with shaky knees,
is like the whole world born again,
with seven unused seas.

If I could start in life again,
I'd want the birds to sing.
I would pick my birthday so
that it would come in spring.

Summer Solace

As days grow long and sunlight gets intense,
the air heats up and bakes the ground beneath.
As robins perch there gasping on the fence,
we know that summer has us in her teeth.

Majestic maples stand and meet the sky,
absorbing heat and brightness with their spread
of branches stretching wide, and thick, and high,
as animals come forth to make their bed.

The solace of the cool and darkened shade
of canopy pinned to the azure sky
transforms these hills into a sleepy glade,
just right for creatures sleeping where they lie.

I pray my home's as welcoming as trees,
for those in need of solitude and ease.

That Time of Year

The pumpkin sparkles diamonds
from the frost kissed by the sun.

The days start growing shorter,
and put summer on the run.

The air is crisp and fragrant
with the smell of changing leaves.

Kid's noses turn to rubies
as they wipe them on their sleeves.

The trees transform from somber green
to radiant red and gold.

The north wind starts to bluster
as it turns our world all cold.

There is a day of which I speak,
which comes but once a year.

Anticipation and excitement
run neck to neck with fear.

Children pace with nervousness
as they wait for dark to fall.

Of all the evenings in their lives,
this is the scariest of all.

There will be no flying broomsticks,
no terrifying creatures.

This is the night that's put aside
for parents to meet with teachers!

Tree of New Beginnings

As I contemplate the approaching year,
with friends all around and my cup of cheer,
I wonder, if I were to become a tree,
which would be the epitome of me?

An evergreen whose leaves never fall,
would be a proud choice, if I recall.
Steadfast, steady, and never-ending,
with branches stout and never-bending.

I try to forge on, with no back-sliding,
face to the wind, my time abiding.
Patient, faithful, and always green.
Whether I'll succeed remains to be seen.

Am I better suited as a deciduous tree?
Just how would I look? Which would I be?
Would my leaves be broad, and offer shade?
In autumn, would I decorate the glade?

Am I the type who would start anew?
Would I shed my leaves as the cold wind blew?
Would I rest dormant through the howling storm,
awaiting the kiss of the sun's rays warm?

Would sap trickle slowly as air grew mild,
to be born again, as a newborn child?
Would new leaves unfurl to embrace the light,
to open wide when the time was right?

As summer came, and the sun shone hot,
would I spread my shade and provide a spot
for forest creatures to seek solace there,
beneath my branches but within my care?

It matters not, be I tree or man,
as long as I follow The Father's plan.
I'll strive to perform each special task
that I've been given, and I will not ask…

"What's in it for me?" I've no need to know.
I am richly paid, when I feel the glow
of my Father's smile upon my heart,
when I know I've done my own small part.

Winter Tantrum

As naked branches tremble in the cold,
the snowstorm roils and boils with angry shouts.
The mighty trunks of oaks will have to hold
their place against the winds and have no doubts.
The woodland creatures burrow deep in dens,
As shrieking windstorms snort, and shout, and sneeze.
The snow piles high and white upon the glens,
Where wind chills dip, and those outside will freeze.

The winter season has one saving grace,
that helps us through the time of ice and snow.
Soon warming sun will come to take its place,
So every living thing can play and grow.
When winter gets you down and feeling low,
go out and make a snowman in the snow!

SECTION 4
Faith

Faith plays a significant role in my life. Without faith, hope, and determination, I would not have progressed so much after my stroke. I believe God is everywhere; I experience His presence at home, in nature, in family, friends, even strangers. We all possess the light of God – some simply shine brighter than others. I want my light to shine through words He gives me to write and through actions I take and thoughts I think. His grace and mercy are new every day, and for that, I am grateful.

God and Nature

God and nature, inextricably bound,
where there is One, the other is found.
How could one doubt the existence of God,
while walking hills graced with goldenrod?

I walk along paths in this city of mine,
my dog at my side, feeling wonderfully fine.
The air is so soft, as it breathes in my face.
Never could other than God make this place.

Others may question, others may doubt.
Perhaps they've not taken this glorious route.
A stream flows softly, leading me on.
My heart-song lingers long after I'm gone.

My mind is easy when I'm submerged
in nature allowing my soul to be purged.
The greatest gift to mankind I could give
is a walk with God as a way to live.

Eye-to-Eye With God

I've often wished I were a tree
that towered to the sky.
I'd peer above the mountaintop,
and greet God eye-to-eye.

To be as mighty as a pine,
above all to prevail,
would be the greatest kind of 'rush,'
to never have to fail.

I've wandered over forest floor,
my eyes in worship raised.
Oh, how I loved their lofty looks,
their majesty I praised.

One day I happened to look down,
and spied a sapling tree
that wasn't big, or strong, or tall,
just eye-to-eye with me.

Pity filled my heart to full,
at such a puny sight.
Its trunk was thin, its branches few,
It lacked the big tree's might.

I understood just how it felt,
I could not measure up.
My job was gone. I had no work.
I felt like a whipped pup.

But then, as I stood looking on
the sapling seemed to grow.
It raised its branches to the light
and challenged any foe.

I marveled at its show if force.
It seemed so brave and sure.
The courage of that baby tree
was Ivory Soap-like pure.

All at once I saw myself
as mighty as a tree.
It mattered not if I was weak,
if I believed in Me!

I feel as tall as any pine,
as strong as any oak.
God bends down to greet small me,
and treats me as kinfolk.

If you feel less than you would like,
don't grieve, don't pine, don't cry.
Just stand up tall, lift up your head,
and look God in the eye!

Angels in Disguise

We're the weaker sex, the gentler sex,
the sex put on Earth to serve.
At the same time we're the enduring sex,
with iron in every nerve.

To us is given the sacred trust
of providing a place in the womb,
for God's children to be brought forth,
in bodies, so their spirits can bloom.

Into our arms each child is placed,
by God, to be raised up right.
We shape and sculpt each unformed soul,
to shine forth its golden light.

In the nests we build, our families live,
kept safe from the storm without.
We keep the walls strong, the roof we mend,
blocking out the rains of doubt.

Our families grow on food we prepare,
so their bodies are nourished and healthy.
We may not be rich in the things of this Earth,
but in spirit we truly are wealthy.

Our foremost reason for time on Earth,
is to carry a guiding light,
for the next generation of Our Lord's souls.
May our lanterns keep burning bright.

In service to all mankind God knew
He could count on each female servant.
Earthbound angels, sisters, women,
who would work with a zest most fervent.

We minister to the needs of the world,
bringing comfort to one another.
You may think you're commonplace,
but to me, you are mankind's mother.

Humbly sisters, we'll pray for the strength
to master each task the Lord gives.
For only then, can we serve Him well,
and enter the gates where He lives.

Country Cemetery

The music of silence
sings for all who rest below.
The only sound, the winds
as through the grass they blow.

Those who come to visit
may tarry for a while.
Breathing in the peace they feel
is sure to make them smile.

Love and contentment
flow through these grounds.
There is no sound of grieving,
for happiness abounds.

Just like the wildlife
that calls this ground home,
Those gone before find sanctuary,
with no urge to roam.

When my life on Earth is done,
and it's time to lay me down.
Just place me in a grave right here,
nearby this tiny town.

God's Plan

The road ahead might not be what you think.
Perhaps you're teetering on the brink.
Do not despair. Don't give up hope.
It's God's way of assuring that you can cope.

Your soul shines through, so bright and clear,
I know God needs you and holds you near.
The task He has for you will take much strength,
To prepare you, He must go to every length.

Your trials, so heavy, have weighted you down.
Don't let them make you bitter, nor make you frown.
Rejoice that God has such trust in you,
That he holds a great service for you to do.

If life slipped by you with nary a trial,
And all He asked of you was to wear a smile,
You'd know He considered you useless and weak.
Of such sadness, I hardly can speak.

As each new trial is laid in your path,
Don't think God angry. Don't fear his wrath.
Just remember, He's preparing your way,
So you can give back, some future day.

Perhaps the places where you've had to live,
Were so you would have understanding to give
to other poor souls who have lost their way,
Who need to be led toward a brighter day.

Reach out to others who might seem lost.
Perhaps right into your path they're tossed,
Because you're the only one able to see
How lost they are, and how very needy.

God doesn't expect us to sail through life,
With never a worry, nor without strife.
Just remember He loves you, and counts on you
To provide the service no one else can do.

Try not to worry, when things go askew.
Just ask the Lord what he wants of you.
If you can listen, and hear His voice,
You'll realize that YOU were his very best choice!

I believe you are one of God's chosen few,
Who go through this life with so much to do,
That you must be readied, and you must be tried,
So that when the time comes, you can be our guide.

God doesn't care what has gone before.
It makes no difference, be you rich or poor.
I'll try to support you, and help you stand.
And when I get lost, I'll reach for your hand.

Seeing-Eye God

The blind put their faith in a seeing-eye dog,
to guide them along life's dark path.
Their dogs keep them safe from the rocks underfoot,
and find shelter to dodge the storm's wrath.

Must those who are sighted endure life alone,
with no helper to guide them along?
If, in despair, you believe this is true,
then friend, you are blessedly wrong!

There is One, who for every soul found on this Earth,
is just waiting to guide over land,
that's so riddled with pitfalls to trip us all up,
that we need to reach out for His hand.

Soul-ward Bound

God cried tears of joy as he looked down
at the raft full of women who were soul-ward bound.
Peace and tranquility would be their reward,
and perhaps a closer walk with his son, their Lord.

He knew the river they travelled upon
was a work of beauty to rival the dawn.
The bluffs of deep red that bordered the path
were so glorious they toppled Satan's wrath.

The current propelled them ever downstream
to landscapes surpassing an artist's dream.
Hearts would be cleansed and minds put at ease
by the rush of water and a gentle breeze.

The river sang a song millennium old,
and whispered secrets that warmed the cold.
The women, all writers, heard the whispered tale
and put it to paper so it would prevail.

Forever buried deep in each woman's heart,
lays a piece of Heaven with which they'll never part.
The river holds each of them in its thrall
as if they had never left its presence at all.

The Rainbow Bridge

(my version)
In Honor of Pookie

I entered the glen with an ache in my heart.
My dear friends and I had been so long apart
Life on this earth just wasn't the same.
I thought of them all; each face, and each name.

The sun shone so brightly that warm summer day.
Though happiness beckoned, I was too sad to play.
I wandered on tiredly, no spring in my step.
I was drained of all energy, sparkle or pep.

I topped a small knoll, looking down on a stream.
A bright rainbow rose, as if out of a dream.
It crossed in a bridge, and silently beckoned.
I didn't know why, but I'd try it I reckoned.

Below me a meadow was teeming with dogs,
Cats, rabbits, guinea pigs, frogs....
Every creature that had once been a friend,
To a person who'd loved them, clear up to the end.

I stared in amazement at the wonderful sight.
Not one single animal suffered a plight.
Each was imbued with vigor and health,
And love abounded, beyond man's greatest wealth.

Suddenly a head bobbed up from the crowd.
He looked so magnificent, stately and proud.
A yip of joy rose from out of his throat.
He sped toward me, with his satiny coat.

It took but a moment for me to see,
He was headed on a collision course with me.
I bent down, beckoning with welcome embrace,
To one who'd passed on with such pain on his face.

The pain and infirmity now were replaced!
With vitality, joy, and tears we embraced.
As we tumbled and wrestled as we had long ago,
I could have him, and love him, and never let go.

As we frolicked, I glanced to the top of the glade.
For a moment the sight made me almost afraid.
A whole mob of critters were racing my way,
What I realized gave me my most glorious day.

Each beloved friend whom I had bidden goodbye,
On the anguished day when he had to die,
Was waiting for me right here in this place,
With happiness, health, and love on his face.

I stood up surrounded by my most precious crowd.
They floated around me like a furry cloud.
The Rainbow Bridge I had seen from above,
We crossed over to happiness and everlasting love.

The death of a loved pet is very hard to bear,
But you'd know it was worth it if you had been there.
I thank the Dear Lord for every pet I've lost,
because I know in the end, it's worth every cost.

Well- Being

Swathed in the languor of morning,
newly risen from out of my bed,
I am flanked by two faithful bassets,
each snug with my hand on its head.

My home wraps itself all around me,
shields me and mine from the storm.
It battles the tempest without,
while keeping me safe and warm.

I study the view from my window.
Golden aspen leaves quake in the tree.
They skitter and skip down the driveway,
as if they were dancing for me.

As rain starts to splatter the window,
and runnels a path down the pane,
I can almost feel arms surround me,
as my Father shields me again.

How often I've welcomed His presence,
and felt His all-abiding love.
I know He is here right beside me,
not watching aloof from above.

"Dear Lord, how I cherish your presence,
take comfort in feeling you near.
I know that whenever I need you,
You'll be waiting beside me, right here.

Amen

ECHOES OF NATURE

About the Author

Bonnie R. Sargent began writing as a child, creating poetry before she could spell. She worked for several years as an elementary school teacher until a stroke happened in 1996. She's crafted memoir, poetry, children's fiction, and inspirational work. Bonnie has won various awards, and Wyoming Writers, Inc., awarded her the prestigious Emmie Mygatt Award for outstanding service to the state-wide organization. She desires to create and publish inspiring articles, stories, and poems to help others who experience hardships. Bonnie is also a supporter of pet rescue and adoption, having volunteered for several years with Wyoming Bassett Hound Rescue. Her current rescue dog, Buzz, provides companionship and inspiration. Visit Bonnie's website where you can read additional poems and her "Ramblings" at https://bonniesargentwriter.pubsitepro.com/

Author photo by Gayle M. Irwin.

About the Book

Writers enjoy varied inspirations for their work. For Bonnie R. Sargent, those motivations include nature, animals, family, and faith. Journey along with her through pristine forest meadows, along rivers and streams, and through courtyards of gardens where you'll meet many animals that have touched her life, including rescue dogs. This collection of poetry will take you into Wyoming, Yellowstone and Teton national parks, and along the Colorado River in the southwestern area of the United States. You'll encounter various wildlife species, such as hummingbirds, chipmunks, ducks, and a pesky mosquito! The author's humor shines within several of her poems. Brace yourself for some epic ponderings along this literary journey!

Made in United States
Orlando, FL
08 August 2024